First Refuge

First Refuge

Poems on social justice

Selected and introduced by Ann Nadge

First Refuge: Poems on social justice
ISBN 978 1 76041 141 1
Copyright © individual contributors 2016
Cover image: *Fold* by Luke Elwes (Own work) [Public domain],
via Wikimedia Commons

First published 2016 by
Ginninderra Press
PO Box 3461 Port Adelaide 5015 Australia
www.ginninderrapress.com.au

Contents

Introduction	Ann Nadge	9
Woomera – Refugees' Day Out…	Helene Castles	11
The bird leaves its cage…	Rob Walker	12
Omega Three…	Jen Gibson	13
Man On a Bus	Danny Gardner	14
No Country For Young Men	Margaret Collett	15
The White Room	Janette Dadd	16
Writing Workshop	Sharon Kernot	17
Real Drone	Tim Metcalf	18
Prisoners of the sun	Gordon McPherson	19
Pay back	J V Birch	20
West Africa	Jean McArthur	21
A piece of stone	Hazel Hall	22
The Fall	Maurice Whelan	23
Themis and her fortune	Ron Barton	24
Cars	Adrian Lane	25
The Recruit	Geoff Page	26
The Ship Breakers of Bangladesh	Joan Fenney	27
Suburban ballad	Valerie Volk	28
Flowers	Annette Herd	29
Refuge	Brenda Saunders	30
The Killing Fields of Cambodia	Jennifer Chrystie	31
Neighbours	Margaret Fensom	32
Stories from the Shoreline, July 1840	Angelee Theodoros	33
That's all you can do	Libby Sommer	34
Identity	Ros Schulz	35
Watercolour Sketches Canberra	Suzanne Edgar	36
Mental Health System	Kate Deller-Evans	37
An Anniversary of Mabo	Stuart Rees	38
Flight	Jill Gower	39
Body Bags	Mark Willing	40
The Refugee's Love Song	Judy Dally	41
Adult Education	Jacqueline Buswell	42

The Sliding Doors of the Supermarket	Russell Erwin	43
Straitjacket Blues	Mary Pomfret	44
Young Rosellas	Ray Carmichael	45
Dislocations	Liam Guilar	46
Report from a Besieged Town	Susie Utting	47
Australia Felix	William Cotter	48
If This Was Peace!	Max Merckenschlager	49
We Were At Peace	Jacqui Merckenschlager	50
Domestic Violence	Dawn Bruce	51
The Demoniser's Song	Alan Gould	52
Grace versus the Highway	Jude Aquilina	53
A Hard Look	Prithvindra Chakravarti	54
Homeless	jenni nixon	55
News Item from Baghdad	Thérèse Corfiatis	56
Breaking Down Barriers	Dawn Colsey	57
Ash Garden	Kathleen Bleakley	58
Borders	Adèle Ogiér Jones	59
Sing Your Landay	Moya Pacey	60
A Question of Justice	Eileen Jones	61
this poem is about silence	Colleen Keating	62
Lament	Anne Collins	63
The Reading Group	Fran Graham	64
Land Lines	Michele Fermanis-Winward	65
The Ghan (Afghan) Then and Now	Roger Furphy	66
A Gully Memoir	Ray Clift	67
Charity	Brendan Doyle	68
Seekers of Asylum	Dale Ashton	69
We continue…	Barbara Gurney	70
To Live Without Honour	John Leonard	71
a day in the life of…	Avril Bradley	72
she wants it to be undone	Sandra Renew	73
The Nightmarkets	Ian C. Smith	74
Spray Can Gran	Nance Cookson	75
Injustice on Justice…	Margo Poirier	76
Song of Athenian Gypsies	Jena Woodhouse	77
Chloe	Elaine Barker	78

Lost Voices	Annette Jolly	79
Disability/invisibility	P.S. Cottier	80
They Came From Elsewhere	Lorna Thrift Brooks	81
Asylum Seekers	Ian McFarlane	82
The Branch	Stefanie Bennett	83
Generations Lost	Myra King	84
Fruit Pickers Calling	Adrian Rogers	85
Down the Rabbit Hole With Alice	Adriana Wood	86
With the Dusk	Antonia Hildebrand	87
The Woman from the Shelter House	Jules Leigh Koch	88
Tutu's Fragments	Ann Nadge	89
Misogynist Myth	Jill Nevile	90
The Eyes Have It	Alice Shore	91
Mental Illness – its vagaries	Brenda Malcolm	92
That Box For Bones	Rodney Williams	93
Social Justice?	Bobbie Barclay	94
Honour	Tracey-Anne Forbes	95
Celebrating May Day	Eileen Haley	96
When My Eyes No Longer See What Happened?	Rose Helen Mitchell	97
	Brenda Eldridge	98
Afterword	Stephen Matthews	99

Introduction

Country of first asylum, or first refuge, is usually a neighbouring country to which a refugee flees.

In the face of great challenge, even reported challenge, writing often becomes the place of first refuge for poets as they seek to make sense of experience and to express their interpretation and reaction. Rilke expresses it in this way:

> Everything conspires to silence us,
> partly with shame
> partly with unspeakable hope.

From the silence and first refuge, emerge art, music, poetry and enduring story. In community, these have the power to lead us from isolation to a place where we can wrestle with words and, in time, enlarge our perspectives on life itself. It is enough, even, to tolerate silence, mystery and uncertainty and to know the limits of words.

In preparation for Ginninderra Press's twentieth anniversary, poets from around Australia were invited to submit poems on the theme of Social Justice. Beyond the notion of GP's anniversary, Stephen Matthews was keen to capture and create a record of the social justice issues that, at this time in history, bring shame and hope to Ginninderra Press poets nationwide.

Some of the poems in this collection have been published previously and others were written during the four-months submission period. We are aware that many poets saw the submission process as a challenge in responding to world news as it unfolded during this time. Seamus Heaney reflected on the process of being in this state of first refuge:

> Now, to pry into roots. I rhyme to see myself, to set the darkness echoing.

The reader will thus experience work from poets whose first refuge was brief; for others, the issue has been of deep concern for years or even decades and the process has prompted them to write.

Rather than organise the book into sections, the decision was made to lead the reader through a range of social justice issues in the way that we become exposed to them – that is, randomly and usually without warning. From the first refuge of the poets' writing processes have emerged poems on Indigenous issues, refugees, domestic violence, homelessness, poverty, the environment, child protection, political oppression, war and discrimination on grounds of race, mental health, disability and sexuality.

Often the poems prompt us to consider what is within our power to change. Auden reminds us,

> Poetry makes nothing happen
> What poetry makes visible is what changes the world

By grappling through the first refuge of writing, poets make things visible to themselves as new perspectives emerge and they often become aware of what Rowan Williams refers to as their 'undefendedness' or vulnerability. In a sermon on poetry and prophecy, on Shakespeare Sunday, 23 April 2006, Williams spoke of

> the acceptance of the wound, the resolve to live with one's own un-defendedness so that certain things in the human world are never forgotten or reduced.

The most powerful of the poems in this collection recognise and express an awareness that social justice is not about 'them', or 'us' but 'me'. They are about global, national, community and personal vulnerability.

As Julie Birch writes in 'Pay back' in this collection,

> their faces loom large
> like dreams with muddy feet
>
> you can't stare too much
> or you'll have to give them things.
> Not just your purse
> but all you are
> so they can take over your life
> and be.

Ann Nadge

Woomera – Refugees' Day Out At the Animal Park

Sulphur crest preened to a single strand
He flipped his head to the side
Held flat as a landed penny
One black eye staring, wide.

Quizzical he acknowledged me,
Cracked seed with a foraging beak.
The cockatoo greeting, I said 'Hello!'
And waited for him to speak.

He turned to the back of the sterile cage
Ignoring the wild bird's cries,
Saw loneliness strut through the quivering gums
And spread to clear blue skies.

Kick to kick while the guards stood watch
The dark-haired boys at play,
The green grass soft in this desert town,
They're released from the dust for a day.

'Abba!' he said and 'Dancing Queen!'
He turned to his friend by his side
Together they laughed in their native tongue
And in our language we cried.

'Why in a cage? Like us!' he said,
With the same dulled look in his eyes.
Futility filtered through shimmering gums
Flung clouds to beautiful skies.

Helene Castles

The bird leaves its cage and enters another

for Juan Garrido-Salgado*

1990.
english was in the air.
the air
was english
blowing on a sea breeze at henley or glenelg
one sentence floats near you

but it will not come
into your mouth

tortured   barred
in & from   your homeland

mute in the newland
your heart bleeds metaphors
exiled from your tongue

alien vowels/consonants
fill your ears
elude your mouth

your heart an injured bird
one wing
plastered to tarmac
an impotent flapping
in Spanish

Rob Walker

---

* In 1990 Juan was granted asylum in Australia after fleeing Chile's Pinochet régime, which burned his poetry and imprisoned and tortured him.

Omega Three...

      you're not for me.
Round wounds
giant ringworms, circular protuberances, harass the Southern Ocean,
   form chain links:
        three,   four,   five,   more
There's life within these circles – herded like cattle to an abattoir
Atlantic salmon
aliens here, encircled in mesh, grow big for slaughter, feed
on alchemical nutrients (pesticidal, antibiotic) –
never experience the joys of free fish.
Underwater homelands shrink
sweet vegetation withers in layers of detritus (destructive effluents)
tiny native fish, shiny black barnacles, local salmon, sea lions
entangle in nets, sicken or die.

Omega three you're not for me.

Atlantic salmon   (to supply Peking and Salamanca)
parade, dressed, on refined al fresco tables; smoked, grilled, baked
prepared in mornay, prepared à la carte.
Crushed fish bones – so much fish oil
seeps from these poor, farmed creatures to
      supply our booming trade
Omega three   heart health for land-based bipeds
Omega three   for healthy-hearted humans...

Despoiling this pristine Southern Sea
we produce rich capsules   of slavery.

Omega three you're not for me.

Jen Gibson

Man On a Bus

(Charles Perkins, riding the Freedom Bus, 1965, two years before Aboriginals were made citizens of Australia and given the vote.)

I have a right to sit on this bus.
I have a journey to make.
I am trying not to watch everyone who is getting on and off.
I have a right to sit here.
There's nothing more natural
than a citizen, needing to be somewhere else,
taking a bus.
If any man or woman sits down beside me
I will welcome them
as a people that has been walking, wandering too long.
And it's not just my pride
or my eagerness to prove a point
that says: none of us belong in a cage.
And it doesn't matter
thinking of Martin Luther King, as you do at this time,
whether the example is
from my neighbourhood
or the other side of the world.
We all, surely, speak the same language on this.
I have a right to be on this bus.
I'm just going to relax,
look out this window
and enjoy the sights.

Maybe I should check to see who is in the driving seat…

I just hope I'm not the only one
left on this bus
when it gets to its destination.

Danny Gardner

No Country For Young Men

They should've left me trapped in the bloody car. Jaws of life, my arse. The wrench and shriek of metal, strobes of red and blue you'll be right mate. Fuckin' bullshit. Never be right again. Like that Metallica song: 'I cannot live I cannot die, tied to machines that make me be.' On my door – Grevillea 24 – Brett – and a picture of horses galloping wild-eyed along a beach. Mornings, I'm rolled over, strapped in, lifted and lowered like a bloody ship's cargo. Jenny and Bev get to punch my pillows wipe my bum stand back aim the shower slap my face with the soapy cloth thread me through my clothes while they rehash their weekend '… and then some idiot bumped me and I spilled beer down the front of that new black top.' Everywhere the tv braying. The oldies shuffle along to Bingo: number 29 in your prime, legs 11, number 13 unlucky for some. Always the stuffy stink of faded lives, spinach slop, air freshener. Old Herb lurches in on his walker to tell me another dirty joke but he can never remember the punchline. I am the punchline. In my mouth a bitter curd. My dreams stain the day like a pissed-in bed. 'Please make your way to the foyer. The bus will be leaving for the mystery tour in ten minutes.' Bec doesn't come any more. Mum visits. I can still see the burning car behind her eyes. I know she intercepts the get well cards. Dad can't even look at me. Noises off, trolleys rattling, barks of laughter. Today's movie will be *Casablanca*. Some old biddy wanders the corridors clutching her doll and bleating 'Oh, wouldn't it be loverly!' Our doors here are never closed. Unless. I want to howl at my reflection in the night window, hurl myself through it, but have to clench all life inside, eyes brimming like city gutters after a storm. Wish I could drown in my own spit. The sweaty little nurse with the port wine birthmark comes to tuck me, seal me in and turn off the light.

Margaret Collett

The White Room

They sit in their white room comfortable and complacent.
You are not allowed to enter.
They admire their achievements have pride in their position and knowing.
You will disturb their peace.
They re-affirm each other their way is good their mind's clean and clear.
If they see your shadow – no admission will be made.
They quietly wait for your silent passing.

It is as it is in the white room
their selected history, their skin-toned view
noble and gracious, honest and proud
the people of the white room.

Your history is denied, sacred places defiled
scrubbed out and erased
conquered and defeated ignored and mistreated.

Do not disturb the white room with your ill-health and illiteracy
your unsanitary lives your struggle to survive.
The white room's glare binds your despair
while wealth is placed with wealth on shelves of the white room.

In the white room they warm themselves with smug satisfaction
while you shiver at their door.

Janette Dadd

Writing Workshop

(For Sue and Elizabeth)

We the able-bodied
sit at the table
write our words
in notebooks.
Pencils and pens scratch paper
as we dip and dive
into our imaginations
at speed

while she
in her wheelchair
with her spasm-arms tethered
blinks her words to her carer –
a constant running through
of the alphabet
as they hunt each letter
until a word is formed.

Sometimes only one word is found
sometimes a line
occasionally a paragraph.
But she does not mind
they are her words
and she is heard.

Sharon Kernot

Real Drone

it is clear right away there is something seriously wrong
the body is lying in the dust and there is blood on the stomach

like a fist plunged in and ripped out a handful of gut
here great vessels are leaking, the blood is filling the belly

if I sear the liver it will cease, we will be able to see again
in the diagram the mesentery looks like America

can we turn down the colour?
click on the fluids icon a couple more times

it's an idealistic simulation
the ideal is what we are fighting for

dust clogs the instruments. the stockmarket's shivering
from lack of blood. you'll be a pilot soon enough

a real drone's harder to control. listen!
the weapons dealer's speaking at the meeting

hours at a screen, are you comfortable there?
you can adjust your seat by pulling on the lever

Tim Metcalf

Prisoners of the sun

Mercury has long since fallen
Into that half sky and Venus, barren
Of her mantle, now locks her naked
Face towards the encroaching blaze.
The sky of soundless borders approaches,
Engorged with indigo and scarlet, crowned
With fiery scimitars, like angelic
Mercenaries, surly for pay, awaiting
The tide of dissolution from the sun's
Malign fevers. What species still observes
And remembers, and what their last flower
In song? Will they cavort in medieval
Excess while the executioner
Prepares and the galactic wheel turns?
Their appeal dismissed and dissolving
Into the refractive haze, will
They regret all the catalogue of the world,
All the regiments of colour, all the
Sprawling continents of fable under
The reddening sun? Will they intone with
Celestial frequencies, unknown to the
Stars, of their heroic extinction? Or
Will they howl for more wage cuts and for
Labour reform, and greater economic growth?

Gordon McPherson

Pay back

They gather in groups
watching you.
You wonder what they're thinking
pray they don't move
don't reach out.

They look lost in their fashion
out of sorts
their faces loom large
like dreams with muddy feet.

You can't stare too much
or you'll have to give them things.
Not just your purse
but all you are
so they can take over your life
and be.

J V Birch

West Africa

Saidu sits on bed edge, one leg swinging.
He is twelve, small, save for neck,
swollen to the width of his head – stiff now,
eyes huge with unformed questions.
He wants to go home…walking with his brother
to their Mandinka village
where Mama tends the young ones and Papa
mends fences to keep goats from groundnut crops.
Long dusty miles, as they came two days ago,
past wind-blown debris, tired palms, leafless boabs.
It is Dry Season in the land of the 21-string Kora.
Music, only in his head, screens
other patients' family babbling,
the antiseptic smell of fear.
Yesterday they waited hours in long queues
among brilliant lime-green, hot-pink mothers' dresses
or cerulean blue with matching headscarves.
Brief surgery to find a name for this growing thing.
He will not be fourteen.

Jean McArthur

A piece of stone

People of Aboriginal descent are respectfully advised that this poem contains the name of a deceased person.

Your name is carved upon a piece of stone
in Eltham, where the faithful congregate.
You wander at the other end of home.

Nineteen, you were, when placed here on your own.
Did sickness of the heart prescribe your fate,
a single name carved on a piece of stone?

You met the man who sat upon the throne,
wore white people's clothes, ate from a plate,
but you were lost and wanted to go home.

A curiosity, you could be shown
as proof that kindness helps them integrate.
They carved your name upon this piece of stone.

Two centuries and more your spirit's roamed.
What song lines can this restless air retrace
for Yemmerrawanyea, so far from home?

Let the elders come and take the bones
across the ocean, where your people wait
to carve your totem with a piece of stone…
On the sacred smoke you'll travel home.

Hazel Hall

Yemmerrawanyea (1775–1794) was a member of the Wangal people at the time of the first settlement in Australia in 1788. He and his kinsman Bennelong accompanied Governor Phillip on the voyage back to England in 1793. Yemmerrawanyea became ill, died and was buried in England.

The Fall

Some die a violent death,
uprooted in a storm,
or lose their place in the dead of night,
forsaken and forlorn.
This one's end was peaceful,
the fall quiet and slow,
the moon painted the heavens bright,
earth was all aglow.
I a privileged bystander,
away from the sleeping town,
saw its roots like a set of pulleys,
lever and lower it down.
It moved like an old clock's hand,
travelling from twelve to three,
touched the earth and hushed,
waves on a gentle sea.
As a child I sailed in its branches,
swung from the lowest bough,
its rustling words were magic,
balm to a fretful brow.
Each year on this night I return,
touch its now lichen-green prow,
remember the curtain descending,
grace in that slow final bow.

Maurice Whelan

Themis and her fortune

Themis and her daughter
splash and swim
in the crisp, clear water at Bondi
while the white sand
blows over their scales,
partially burying them.
Australia, the lucky country:
provided your particulars
reflect party policy.
Uncle Sam
might have declared
that all men are created equal
but the Little Boy from Manly
has borrowed Fortuna's blindfold,
not in an effort to remain impartial
but to blind himself
from our misdeeds.
Our boundless plains
are ours alone –
turn back the boats,
incarcerate the indigenous –
while a UN investigation
reveals how unAustralian
we really are.

Ron Barton

Cars

The new cigarettes
Burning resources non-renewable
Choking, killing, maiming
Even those who try to save
By walking, cycling;
Forcing low-density housing
Massive lots, garages, tar over half the earth
Stormwater flooding, wasting, guzzling –
You've no idea how much we pay –
Freeways over farms,
Now taking, eating our food
To fuel our little worlds
That push away:
Addicts never know their smell till clean.

The greatest cities in the world:
London, Paris, New York
All have subways – made great by subways –
Who visits LA?
Everybody loves a tram, a train
Don't underestimate the power – pain – of gas
Be careful lest on looking in the rear
You find it gone:
Congestion up ahead.

Adrian Lane

The Recruit

Every now and then you see him,
replayed on his slice of footage,
somewhere in the opening days –

squat but solid, city hat,
five foot six at best,
cigarette between his fingers

flourishing a wisp of smoke.
He's glancing back towards the camera,
soundless in its shifting greys.

It's not long after six.
Brushed by two hours' worth of schooners,
and three sheets to the wind,

his mates have pushed on through the crowd,
drawn by something in the yeast
or women's whispers just now heard.

Six bob a day, the army says,
and 'Christmas in Berlin'.
'C'mon, mate!' he hears them calling,

Bluey, Jacko, Nobby, Fred.
He waves his cigarette at us;
then turns to join the dead.

Geoff Page

The Ship Breakers of Bangladesh

Shrouded in darkness he pulls on his T-shirt
and shorts, slips on his flip-flops. He is 14
and traipses daily to the beaches of Chittagong
to strip bare the giants of the sea.

Encased in a cloud of smoke and fumes
battered ships and rusted oil tankers pulled
from the ocean seep poisons into the sand.

Sinking into the sludge he joins pallbearers
heaving black cables bound to the wrecks.
His arms bear deep, jagged scars, etched
like tattoos in grime. He can't block the ache
in his ears from exploding oils and metals.

In the shadow of the ships' graveyard
workers hunger to escape the 12-hour days.
At 47 cents an hour dreaming is all they have.

Ripping apart the hulls by hand the sting
of acrid sweat burns his eyes as the caustic
taste of bitter toxins fills his mouth. He dodges
falling shards of steel and burning metal
that have crushed his friends.

Every year thousands of vessels strewn
along the Chittagong coast unite with lost lives
to become ghosts at the water's edge.

Joan Fenney

Suburban ballad

Tonight he carried flowers –
a sight I'd often seen.
Crimson roses – perfect –
a few white ones between.

I watched him through the window
until he reached the door.
His footsteps on the stairwell,
And then I heard no more.

I'd hardly spoken to her
since they had moved in there.
She was a quiet little thing,
blue-eyed, with mousy hair.

But yet he must have loved her,
so often to bring flowers.
I'd turn the TV up quite loud
to fill my evening hours.

Apartment walls are far too thin;
one can hear every sound.
Good neighbours should keep quiet,
not spread their gossip round.

She saw me looking at her
and put dark glasses on.
'I'm really just so clumsy.'
Then she was swiftly gone.

She rarely speaks to anyone;
It's bad the way she cowers.
So sad her words to me: 'I wish
he wouldn't bring me flowers…'

Valerie Volk

Flowers

A poet's response to terrorism in Paris

More powerful than any gun
Are all these flowers here, my son
Laid in respect for those who died
Defying terrorists who tried
To frighten us and make us hate
I'll promise you they'll meet their fate.

As you are sitting on my knee
I beg you, listen carefully
I hope the seeds my words have sown
Will blossom once you're fully grown
And you will be a man one day
Who has no hateful word to say.

Let every race and creed unite
Together we will win this fight
If we agree to walk as one
There will not be a single gun
To threaten or destroy the powers
We have invested in these flowers.

Annette Herd

Refuge

People fear the fireball
spinning towards them
Is it a drone, or a shooting star
flung out of orbit?
Escape hovers at the edge
of the unknown
offers an uncertain future
to those fleeing a present danger

Held in the searchlights
there is no time to think
of freedom
Somewhere along the way
they lose the details
of their lives
Forget the meaning
of belonging

Collect a new self
from scraps
caught on the cyclone wire

Brenda Saunders

The Killing Fields of Cambodia

Bamboo encircles this ragged plot
each pole decorated with a bracelet
in rainbow colours

After decades ravaged
by insect and worm, bones
buried in suffocating soil

move accusingly to the surface
to be harvested and sequestered
in a many-tiered monument

Children were grabbed by the ankles
skulls smashed against the Cannonball tree
or throats cut with razor-edged palm fronds

Many still lived when buried
their thin cries drowned out
by loudspeakers hanging from branches

Tourists try but fail
to understand
Birds and cicadas fall silent

Jennifer Chrystie

Neighbours

Many flowering islands lie
in the waters of wide Agony*

How have I managed to live my life
on a flowery isle?

Would I ever leave to brave stormy seas? Perhaps
if bombs rained on my city or I was sought
by those who seek to persecute my faith.

Sometimes I feel blocked by little things
but greater far the obstacles that block
those on Manus Island or Nauru,
marooned long years in camps for refugees,
those fleeing ruined cities as winter comes:
snow on a land without shelter.

A lawyer once asked,
'Who is my neighbour?'

Margaret Fensom

---

* These lines are from 'Lines Written Among the Euganean Hills' by Percy Bysshe Shelley.

Stories from the Shoreline, July 1840

The opaque sea-mist of uncertainty dissolves at low tide
A lonely isolated beach revealed
Not like the drawing of curtains on a new day
But the lifting of gauze from a festered wound
A smooth large creature bogged motionless in the white sand
Is gently caressed in rhythms of lapping waves
But the baby Southern Right Whale is not comforted
Each shallow breath of life, is a sob
Staring, defeated sad eyes recall the horror
The piercing cry of its mother as sharp as the harpoon
The moan of pain like a thousand ships scraping on unforgiving rocks
Amplified through the depths of endless ocean
The taste and smell of blood flesh and blubber
Spreading a soup of fear with the current
No more nourishment or protection
Just the eternal song of silence
Echoing like parched white driftwood.

Angelee Theodoros

That's all you can do

The news reports:
at watch and act today total fire ban
smoke haze poor air quality asthma sufferers
and other respiratory problems stay indoors.

Hot north westerly winds
west and southwest of Sydney
properties cleared and prepared
an anxious night   distant sirens confusion
to leave or to go?
Springwood, Yarramundi.

Residents report:
rescue our animals and get out of here
a new fire break
it's always your family   that's more important
pack up your photos   that's all you can do
temporary accommodation
photos are what you've seen and experienced.

On amber watch today
200 houses destroyed so far
hoping and praying for the best
containment lines will they hold?

Exhausted fire fighters
people's lives are the most important
fire crews keep back-burning
what else can you do?

Despite ember attacks on homes
Rural Fire Service to link up bushfires as winds drop.

Today has started off cool.

Libby Sommer

Identity

Not just waiting in a queue, living in it
at the border of your neighbor's country
sleeping there, eating – probably not eating at all
defecating – where else?

Do you still clutch the leather wallet
with its cards all gone, as proof
that once you'd had them? Would the thick
woolly overcoat wrap further round each day?

Your face featureless, a screen gone blank,
eyes registering nothing, heart pumping blood
for feelings that have now evacuated;
a grave would mock when a living claim's denied.

But I insult you to presume to know what you feel.
I know only what it's like to not exist
in a room full of people
who don't share my views,
to not rate a thought from someone I care about,
to speak to someone
who is looking past my shoulder
at someone else.

Ros Schulz

Watercolour Sketches   Canberra

W.B. Griffin: 'I have planned an ideal city'

Townscape

I'm near the till in the supermarket queue
behind a dark-skinned girl, we shift our feet
while a darker hand in front shuffles coins,
his five and ten cent hoard…a white palm waits…
He's got enough for fags but not another cent.
'Managed Income!' the check-out lady sniffs.
Our eyes all slide away to the rain outside.

Beneath the eaves of the chic museum of art
a man lies flat on his back across the path,
snug from chin to toe in a sleeping bag.
His 'pillow' of rags is wedged against the wall.
The face is thin and wan, enclosed in sleep.
On the edge of puddled streets he's found a niche,
sheltered from the storm in a makeshift bed.

Driving home around the swollen lake,
I pass a figure fighting the force of the gale,
his black umbrella braced to fend off sleet.
He's short and stout, with an oddly mincing gait.
I stop the car and offer him a lift.
He'd be delighted: 'I go to meet my wife.
She Ambassador, at Embassy, up there.'

Suzanne Edgar

Mental Health System

for adolescents

On the tour of the ward
we're shown the time-out room
where there's just a mattress
minus a base, in the corner,
four walls coloured blue and white
– sky on a cloudy day –
there's no window but for the one in the door
its glass thick in the heavy wood
and I think, Oh no, don't lock me away!
realise it's not me they're admitting
and I say quietly to the nurse,
'You might like to clean
the blood smears from the floor'
and she says, 'Oh yes, I've a few things
to take up with the cleaners but
they won't be happy with me.'
As if this were fine.
As if this were normal.
Or that she was in the wrong
and should apologise to them.

Kate Deller-Evans

An Anniversary of Mabo

In an unexpected dream
it is difficult to tell
whether dawn waters are shining
or decades later
are an illusion from mists
when a few brave justices
recalled a record of the dispossessed
which history said had not happened
until with careful haste
they broke the mindset
of dire predictions
that losers would win and winners lose.

Over the red brown deserts
by picnic spits called table lands,
across the soils of plenty
came a prospect of lands restored
and health revived, as slowly
as self respect could be sketched
in song lines smudged
when languages were lost
and the property men prevailed,
whose descendants now conclude
the Mabo mob should be grateful
for what might happen today
and did not happen then.

Stuart Rees

Refers to the High Court's Mabo decision of June 1992.

Flight

Hungary, September 2015

across vast tracts of land
and treacherous oceans
crammed into ramshackle boats they flee
desperate refugees, asylum seekers
in their thousands
the aged who must be carried
the children who stumble
the babies in arms
the women and men who must be strong
for all of them
they are weary in a way we have never known
hope is all they have to cling to
as they arrive hungry thirsty exhausted
halted by tear gas and barbed wire boundaries
a floodgate built too quickly to keep them out
rejection in its worst form
forced by barbaric soldiers
to run from their own beloved country
or face mutilation rape death
fellow human beings
forced to beg and plead for their lives
in a peaceful country
and yet still again they are defeated

Jill Gower

Body Bags

It's not all one way
traffic here. For every soldier
a body bag complete with vinyl finish
full length zip and six handles
$75 or $150 for the upmarket
olive green heavy duty bag.

They're flying them out
the boys, our children
soldiers of shadow preceding them
a subdued company of vague human shapes
stacked neatly in piles
beside the battle field.

What kind of humanity cloned in vinyl
warranting a price and choice of colour
has come to this? What screwed-up
piece of human logic
anticipates death for its children
and then goes about its dire preparation?

The shadow children will soon come home
zipped to closure, no doubt with respect
and the roar of guns and the whisper of blades
will soon become history's shadow time.
Not so their children in a disposable world
growing more and more so by the minute;
their shape and size already measured at birth
just waiting for fresh orders to respond.

Mark Willing

The Refugee's Love Song

I miss
white cheese
unleavened bread
fresh vegetables
your kisses

I miss
roasted meat
quinoa and rice
fresh spices
your kisses

But I will embrace
the Aussie tastes
of fast food
and barbecue
until I taste
your kisses

Judy Dally

Adult Education

we learn our geography in the narration of war
Dresden   Hiroshima   Chechnya

some places we name carefully
choosing allegiances – Uluru   Malvinas
Palestine

there are place names that sound
as if they figure on a single compass
yet are unrelated and far apart
inner west   middle east   deep south

ethnography we learn from dark stories
of massacres – Dharawal   Tutsi

new lessons in anti-archaeology teach
destruction by blast and smash
no more slow crumble to ruin:

dynamite for the Buddhas of Bamiyan
jack hammers in the temples of Nineveh

blinded by our city lights
we fail in astronomy

we forget the importance of boats
though from wardrobe to workshop
we see the evidence of trade: made in China

in myriad personal encounters
we gauge our resilience and debilities

then growing old, we learn anatomy anew
from the body's growing map of symptoms

Jacqueline Buswell

The Sliding Doors of the Supermarket

It's not just his appearance, drunk, sad case, lost cause,
which causes trolleys to wobble-veer down other aisles,
a mother to regather a toddler, who's wandered off,
for others to construct distance from a stare
but the rasped chanting, like a pruning saw,
which works unstopped into us,
into our soft tissue of fear.

This voice, slurred, is sound, not language, is menace,
is an abyss. There is no point of contact.
It threatens like a wounded animal. No.
It is as alien as one who stands outside
our houses and stares.

His chain-saw of clotted sound rips
silence through the slurry of classic pop songs,
'Calling Michelle. Michelle to the checkout.'
This violence – without humour or object,
without meaning, just venting…

Why do I feel impotence before this ranting,
chanting man, and a kind of guilt,
and a sense of being released
when stepping through the sliding doors
which as they softly shut – 'thut'

– and see a single, ragged plum
in the car park, frosted with blossom,
distinct against the larger, softer expanse of the dusk
as his voice is lost, muffled in there,
scouring between the aisles?

Russell Erwin

Straitjacket Blues

They walk with a shuffle
like convicts in shackles
their speech staccato
they spit out words and teeth
dentists, you know, are for the middle-classes
and pliers are cheap and do the job
medication keeps the head voices quiet
strait jackets no longer necessary
submission comes in a syringe
or a pill bottle
smiles when they come are fleeting
disappearing quickly at the recollection
of not having asked permission.
spontaneous acts are not allowed
could be dangerous
community treatment orders protect
people from themselves
long as you take your meds
don't talk too loud
don't take up too much room
don't pick up butts in the street
don't scare children and old ladies
then you can live out in the community
with the rest of us, the mentally well.
Institutions are a thing of the past aren't they?

Mary Pomfret

Young Rosellas

The young rosellas hush their flying thrill;
clouds have gushed and now are moving on;
crows call and click shut, locked within a suburb;
a native frog, never heard to gulp, is gulping;
and dogs have cooled with silence.
Driveways wait to raise their steamy veil
when wheels return from one day of survival
and night shall fall when families bond tight
to lift a mortgage or to rent in hope
beside the sporting crews who throw their wages in;
some kiss, some bicker, some do both.
They love with passion or announce a theft.
Young rosellas pause, preened to flash the air
now the streets and trees are rinsed.

Ray Carmichael

Dislocations

1

We came across the ocean, towards nightfall
the sunset at our backs stripped colours
from the land. No one was waiting on the quay.

2

...in my case. By coach to Digbeth station.
The terminal stench of City after rain:
damp cloth, upholstery and diesel fumes,
stained our lives and ever after drove us back

again doors hissed contempt, or resignation
and dumped us down amongst discarded ticket stubs.
We struggled through the wash of consonants.
Outside, the only people there without routines,
we could not read the signs.

3

We turned our backs on home:
wind, rain, and sky, the shape of clouds
familiar as an accent calling out

at evening. We landed,
shuffled past the lighted windows,
moved inland, towards sunrise.

Liam Guilar

Report from a Besieged Town

(after Zbigniew Herbert)

I will try to be precise
but I don't know
when the end begins –

already the future here
where houses   whole gardens are dug up   no wooden tombstones
mourn when nothing remains

Dredgers clank –
clank through their teeth singing
mouths full of coal

Our voices are never heard
by bureaucrats in sheepskin suits butchering at midnight
in cabinet yards

Our children run
over bare slabs   chipped
shadows of a nightmare

beyond the levelled corpse
Meanwhile the beast licks itself
clean   of remorse

Overhead a crow
crosses the landfall
where our future empties

into waiting trucks
I will write quietly   so my voice is loud
chirping in the dust

Above the town
cooling crematorium towers
this dark satanic mine.

Susie Utting

Australia Felix

The wedge-tailed eagle comes alone here, now,
The keeper of winters, summers, murders,
The single voice and the passing shadow,
The wing scribbling down the sandstone ridges.
He it was who saw the feeble sun slide
And erase, the darkness spit sudden fire,
The horses on the steepest slopes, the wide
Eyed children desperate to climb higher,

Heard the straggling acacias lamenting,
In the clean, semi-dark caves the cut short cries
Of mothers. The snub nosed shotguns barking
And the hideous game of hide-and-seek.

But all is calm, now. And across the plain
He carries in silence one people's shame, another's pain.

William Cotter

If This Was Peace!

If this was peace
we'd question her presence on a demolition site
we'd determine whether or not
OH&S work requirements were all in place
we'd inquire into the mental state
of both victim and dozer driver
at the time of the incident
we'd seek a report on the mechanical fitness
of the earthmoving equipment

work would pause
out of respect for the deceased
her family and her friends
bilateral outpourings of grief and loss
would be anticipated and natural
civil action might later be considered

but this is not peace
and all is fair, they say
in love and war.

Max Merckenschlager

On 27 February 2003, American peace activist Rachel Corrie was crushed when she stood between an Israeli bulldozer and a Palestinian home.

We Were At Peace

a poem written to complement the painting by E.C. Frome, *On Whitton Bluff*

Because they came in ghostly ships,
spirits from another world,
because we chose to greet new folk
with courtesy and caution,
because our land was bountiful
and they were only few, we let them be.

Because a simple life contented us,
earth and sea providing all,
because we watched with curiosity
their strange and tempting ways,
because we let them live on land
and we were few, they let us be.

Until the white man fenced us out
and treated us like thieves,
until they broke our ancient laws
and scoffed at our traditions,
until they punished us for hunting
on the land we loved, we let them be.

Until our desperation is acknowledged,
we must recount that history,
until injustices are overturned,
we will be hurt and angry,
until the white man and the black
unite to honour country, we must speak out.

We cannot let it be.

Jacqui Merckenschlager

Domestic Violence

you make my world
a web
circling
holding me in place
by invisible forces

you
reach out
draw sticky threads
around and around
me

I struggle
become a tight bundle
enclosing on myself

you wrap me
in a curled leaf
leave me in dim light
until I am still
and ready for your feasting

Dawn Bruce

The Demoniser's Song

I thought my colleague nerveless, snide,
he cosied to the easy side.
I imaged him and I went spare,
but he was coming from elsewhere,
    and stepped aside from my fierce mind.
    Our talk was rich and unrestrained.

I watched the power the shrew accrued,
the things she said so shrewdly cued.
Hateful, except her quick disdain
was flux from her more hidden pain.
    And when we passed upon the stair,
    she smiled and we were equals there.

'The Side of Ricochet,' I quipped,
my sneer obedient to a script
that watched for 'side' with racing pulse.
But what they did was something else
    where for a spell they could let pass
    their quickfire spiels of prejudice.

I saw the banners, red and blue,
fretting my window's equal view.
Loudspeakers bellowed, 'Seize redress.
The demon prospers, you grow less.'
    A further offered, 'Go in peace,'
    nor would enlarge this prompt release
    though he loomed large within redress.

Alan Gould

Grace versus the Highway

Wearing her face like a domett shroud
Grace weaves between days of domestic decay
and nights with Chopin and Strauss.
Inside her ramshackle temple
the bible radio babbles, weevils breed
and last week's apple crumble grows fur.

She watches the buses through parted lace.
After seventy years of service, the tea trolley
creaks no more and the lead crystal is grey.
Her sons are old men in foreign cities
her pets have fertilised the rampart ivy
and the busy street is stranger than TV.

A hanging garden chokes veranda posts,
violets and agapanthus bury the pathways.
Entwined in her nest, Grace is safe for now
until the rats in suits and ties arrive
bearing smiles and papers to sign.
Her shrine will be desecrated by July.

Jude Aquilina

A Hard Look

A bird and a wriggly caterpillar.
A hawk and a young rabbit perhaps…
After adjusting the glasses
And resting his live Havana on the ashtray
(The grey smoke wafting towards the bungalow's roof)
The grand old man in the wheelchair has a hard look:
Ah, it's a perfect match: a rhino of a commando and a novice babbling Che:
He, in an unsavoury attire of his tribesmen, walking about easy
And the defender of the faith twirling his eyes to keep apace.
Must not the tall proud ironwood in the bush dwarf the long grass mob?

The spreading of shadows is a dire duty
But foraging about the bushes and dunes is an adventure.

The special assignee on the sacred oath,
Neatly armed and ever ready on the ground,
Is about to charge at the pest
For an unforgivable act of sabotage.
Doesn't he loosen the basements of our great towers?
Sneak into the factories to disable the engines?
And brainstorm our kids to eliminate the 'unbelievers'?
Damn rascals! The vermin living off the leftovers!

The whole gang of the uncivil chumps
Shall be inundated under the burning lava.
No Noah's Arc will save them from their derelict life
Hanging by the end of a thread of ethereal delusion.

The caterpillar or rabbit or even a robust cobra
Must face the fix-all 'self-loading' saviour's beak,
Ever sharp and hooked,
As long as the outcast acts as a prey.

Prithvindra Chakravarti

Homeless

they cram into tents in Belmore Park.
a million dollars the cost of an average home in Sydney
billions to house asylum seeks off shore.

after the accident   slide down spiral of madness
to cardboard covered by a blanket
dog Bluey by her side.   people say, 'get rid of the mutt.
her only friend barks at danger   warns off strangers.
knife attack took eight dollars made her fear worse.
don't block the footpath   move on.'

   in fifty large cities of the United States
   now a crime to feed street people
   directive from police officer: drop that plate
   Love Thy Neighbour   stop feeding the poor.
   violations carry penalties – $500 fine or 60 days in jail.
   left with no food or coffee   homeless hungry people.

some people think it's god's punishment
destiny or choice
   – make your bed   you lie in it.

head lowered   wipes tears from his eyes
gnaws at his knuckles
homeless veteran of the Iraq war
did tour of duty with honour
came home with post-traumatic stress disorder.
just another derelict   wrapped in a blanket
on the street in Darlinghurst.

jenni nixon

News Item from Baghdad

It's summer in one of the hottest cities on earth,
news footage shows women shaking hoses
to catch last precious drops –
buckets half empty, like drawing water from stone.
Unbearably cruel conditions
no infrastructure rebuilt despite promises sworn.

How has this happened in the land of two rivers
this destruction and carnage
this theft of resources, slow death of a people?

Iraq gave the world its first farmers, irrigation systems
encoded humanity's first laws
invented the wheel and the brewing of beer
used astronomy and astrology
fusing them into the fabric of daily life
and built a tower to heaven
desiring to placate nature and the gods.

They wrote annals on medicine,
possessed doctors who understood
how someone can die of a broken heart,
revered poets and musicians
adored flowers and fine clothing,
distilled perfumes, crafted intricate works of art
built modern cities to equal any today.
We owe them so much for all that we know.

It's summer in one of the hottest cities on earth.
Let them drink sand.

Thérèse Corfiatis

Breaking Down Barriers

at seventy-one
Mary walks with her stick
on Tasmanian snow
to take hand-knitted beanies
to asylum seekers in detention
the note from her knitting group
reads, 'Dear men, we hope that these beanies
warm your heads and your hearts.'

Dawn Colsey

Ash Garden*

Turning the pages of an ash garden – the Battle for Baghdad 2003

Hiroshima 1945: flesh no longer belongs to bodies
lying in American hospitals

The Gulf War 1991/how quickly action is named/a new computer game

Acid rains, the garden grows heads without names, a thousand origami cranes

Charcoal rings around garden beds
promises break & fall in an autumn park
a bronzed arm
on the mantle of peace
golden gifts for the victor

A blackened wall, sixty thousand poppies scattered
the fallen ones, where is the unknown civilian?

These children have suitcases

Gas masks are abandoned

The scent of rosemary & thyme
branding our memory cells

Turn singed pages of an ash garden
we are fed the news, too full to remember
John Wayne gallops into the latest ad break

People behind desks getting fatter/bellies distend
hunger shrieks
children trying to run
not enough water in the desert storm

Sing me a lull-a-lie
stumbling in the halls of forgetting
too dark to read in the ash garden

Kathleen Bleakley

* Title inspired by Dennis Bock, *The Ash Garden*, HarperCollins, 2001.

Borders

Children crossing on solemn journeys
searching work or markets for goods of little worth
see no border marking this place on the ground
no soil of different hue and colour
only posts with words they cannot read
and uniforms proclaiming ownership.

Speaking dialects and tongues
of neighbours through villages and towns
crossing appears the natural thing to do
without a post prohibiting, preventing
journeys their fathers and those before them made
no hesitation or attention to what officials declared
like seeds of sunflowers
blown in the wind, warmed only by sun.

As bees touch down for single songs
flying off to find new nectar sweet at sunset
children see no sense to halt at borders
except to escape the frown and rule imposed
deportation to where their language is most known
though they speak them all with ease.

Children crossing on weary trekking
families resting on their backs
school experiences the day provides
learning keeps them strong for days to come,
no need of borders imposed outside them
no danger greater than family loss
waiting, expecting sons to join their fathers
lost to other lands, ground which claimed them long before.

Adèle Ogiér Jones

Sing Your Landay

In the dark cage of the village
a woman's voice sings of the girl
who stole her brothers' honour.
They shaved her black curls,
closed her green eyes, scooped
the body into a sack –
threw it into the cold river.

Come back into the world
girl with black curls and green eyes.
Put on your wedding shoes.
Let your hennaed fingers
beat the hand drum.
Sing your landay –
over and over.

Moya Pacey

A Question of Justice

Our migrant ancestors
fought oppression, drought, fire, flood.

Now,
in our freedom-loving country
asylum seekers, lost souls
locked behind razor wire,
to be returned to the oppressive regime
they tried to escape.

Australians trapped overseas,
isolated by official silence,
pawns in the game
of international politics,
are detained without trial
indefinitely.

We turn a blind eye,
succumb to the temptation
to placate powerful allies.

Is there only one Cornelia Rau?
Only one David Hicks?

Eileen Jones

this poem is about silence

words get in the way of silence
it needs a blank page
it needs space
in silence there can be longing
there can be anticipation
intimate or hostile

you can hear it
in the pin-drop moment
between bow and string

you can feel it between breaths

the inarticulate uses violence
for expression
is this silence?

when one turns their back
their silence is palpable
and what of silence imposed in fear?
anonymity is powerful and loud

a silent protest is loud

when the powerless stitch their lips together
with needle and fishing line
is this silence
even as tears fall?

a poem about silence
needs to be loud
to be heard

Colleen Keating

Lament

After the film *All the Invisible Children* (excerpt from a suite of poems)

A group of boys in rags
clutch assault rifles, move
through fields of lush green maize.
The sun heats their fears,
they wait, watch, then shoot
other boys coming towards them
in crisp khaki camouflage.

Ekene surveys the enemy's village,
from a hilltop,
neat mud huts and skipping girls below.
He follows orders,
breaks padlocks at night,
steals into classrooms with bombs,
reads tomorrow's questions on the board,
writes chalk answers, pleased
he knows the capital of France is Paris.

Sitting at a desk,
Ekene falls asleep in tears,
dreams
of a time before he was kidnapped.

Anne Collins

The Reading Group

I had really enjoyed the novel.
It had substance
and wonderful characters
survivors mostly
a spinster, a couple of crazies
an amputee, an over-zealous priest
and a homosexual.

The discussion moved along nicely.
Then – Freaks! she said
They're all freaks!
I want to read about normal people.

I was just beginning to like her
when she vomited this up.
In my quest for like-minded
women one can trust
she suddenly didn't rate.

As she seemed such an expert on freaks
and their unsuitability to be characters in novels
I decided not to mention I had
a daughter with mental illness
two damaged brothers
a son-in-law in a wheelchair
a disability myself
and that I was a lesbian.

As I left the café
I struggled to stay upright
under the weight of my disappointment.

Fran Graham

Land Lines

Does an arbitrary line drawn on a map
exist today, beyond police and guns,
the limits of a politician's heart
they call our national pride?

Tribes were broken by the ruling class
when carving land as spoils of war.
Now TV screens and mobile phones
eclipse old border posts.

I watch nature under siege
and squander riches others crave.
My forebears stole this land
when they denied its native claims.

Do I have rights above the crowd
who have nowhere to call a home,
who cry their need to work and live,
a land that's safe from harm?

Michele Fermanis-Winward

The Ghan (Afghan) Then and Now

before the Ghan they were camel drivers
Middle Eastern Muslims peeling the edges
of desert life to distant outposts
their rugs at night to an eastern sky
and generations on through Europe
Afghanistan, Iraqi, and Syrian refugees
from ancient lands on boats to Greece
and trains on through overwhelming
a reluctant EU generous in moral reserve

now a new Ghan reaches north, south
stencils diesel stamp on parallel lines
and sleepers where dreaming clicks rhythm
on flicker of mirage or imagination
leaning from doors staring from windows
I see them to the fringes of rural revival
new life our sharing an empty land
until awake to the lie of our parochial land
another day.

Roger Furphy

A Gully Memoir

I remember Johnny Ryan
With his Modbury pub
I remember cool green grass
When families frolicked
At the Highbury listening to the bands
I remember all the hoo ha
When the Blue Gums band rang out
I remember flooded fords
With bubbling rushing streams
Across the Ladywood
Where vineyards thrived for years
But that was long ago
When progress made us catch our breath
And trapped us in its vice.

Ray Clift

Charity

Twenty-five dollars a month.
Tax deductible?
Now you're talking.
To put a face on a smile
– Yes, I did see it on TV –
in an African village.
A personal touch.
Yes, I'm sure we can afford it.
Oh, I have to write to them as well?
Maybe the kids can do that.
Good for show and tell.
A cheque will do?
Ah, direct debit from my account.
Excellent. That way,
I won't even have to think about it
any more.

Brendan Doyle

Seekers of Asylum

a boat drifting at sea on calm water
a small boy asks his father how long
talking softly with his foreign tongue
interest stirs as land is sighted far off

until a lone coastguard boat arrives
through barbed wire Ahmed watches
children walking on the way to school
behind the huts line up like Lego blocks

crying women and angry men caged
outside the fence, different colours
and strange stars in the night sky,
but everything else in the compound

is what they had left behind them
across the road Abby watches the boy
behind the barbed wire after her dad
said he would take her job one day

but from here he just looks very sad
feeling guilty, but not really sure why,
she runs the rest of the way to school,
where she learns about the lucky country

Dale Ashton

We continue…

Trees obliterated by society
Flora uprooted for unconcerned residents
Stubbled ground cleared with unsympathetic authority

No one protests
Over one small acre
Why care?

but…

Lost:
A bobtail's home
Not harming
Just being
For immeasurable time

now…

Pattering over hot bitumen
Away from noise; in terror
A refugee from destruction
Scurrying for cover
Amid superficial borders
Trimmed edges
Cultivated roses

He can't go back

and yet
we continue…

Barbara Gurney

To Live Without Honour

To live without honour altogether
Is to wake each morning with a sour taste
In the mouth, to go about knowing
That your work is not for the good
Of people, or the world, to know
That honour once given up
In words and actions, generally,
Is hope gone, the future dangerous.

Even when the way seems plain,
Goldfinches flying about your head,
It is to no end, leads to
No trust, or possession to pass on.
Honour given up is to have
People cast their strength away.

John Leonard

a day in the life of…

overnight

He jumps the fence to lie beneath
Norfolk pines; needled like them he needs
their shelter. He's done time chasing after
soup and blankets. In the distance
a prick of ocean shivers up the sky.
In a cold tremble he waits for

a new start

Hanging about on the last margin of yesterday,
dawn comes up with a blank page.
He signs his name. A name he doesn't use.
No one uses his name. It lives on
a government form; to be considered.
The library is open. He reads rumbles of his hunger.

afternoon delight

He scours damp streets. Combs the bins for
life support, something to munch. He watches
traffic seam past in an unbroken thread of
others' lives

nightfall

Too cold for the pines, he roams the playground
shunned by anxious mothers soon to go home.
He waits. Hunkers down in the cubby house
hidden from view. Shrouded in the discomfort of
his future.

Avril Bradley

she wants it to be undone

the silence
about our life
together
because we cannot marry
is only silent in law

she wants it to be undone
the argument about the word – this specific word – their mouths opening
and closing the noise bursting and crashing
so loud she cannot hear it
so loud she cannot bear it
she feels behind her eyes the tsunami vibrating in the teacup
feels under the soles of her bare feet the veranda floorboards shrieking
under the heavy work boots
she wants it all to be undone
and now whatever was between the boy and his father
depending on the words and even if they could start the day again
as the anger and shame
gusts and buffets
whatever is between them, the father will be accosted by his mates in the
pub with the word, the son will feel the danger behind him in the street   feel
the word assaulting him in shouts and taunts

to change minds
we try words and try words again
words sharp as metal
when a book becomes a gun…
do you want a gun?

Sandra Renew

The Nightmarkets

Beyond our rear fence his wan light glows,
all-night radio softly keeping jitters company
whenever I arrive back late from wickedness.
I piss on rank weeds in this tiny backyard
facing his shed, his asylum, hear him sigh,
wrestling memories that refuse to die.

My landlady said he lived on a TPI pension
sipping beer all night long behind his sister's house
where trains still curve before rumbling beneath the road,
an ex-POW who could never forgive his tormentors.
I was a boy, so young, so poor,
my spirit kindred with a man I never saw.

Ian C. Smith

Spray Can Gran

Mervyn's grandma does grafitti
Mervyn's grandma, what a hoot
You'd never think she had it in her
There she stands in that tweed suit.

Mervyn's grandma got arrested
Caught red-handed near the bridge
Scrawling slogans with a spray can
like a kid that's on the edge.

Old age didn't stop the sentence
In the court the judge was stern
'You,' he said, 'you're no example
to the young on how to learn.'

His attitude was regimental
He treated grandma to a sneer
That was anything but sentimental.
'Get this vandal out of here.'

Mervyn's grandma's doing time
She believes that war's obscene
She says that everyone's entitled
To fulfil at least one dream.

Sending youth to far-off battle
Long before their dreams ignite
Is a dangerous occupation
Grandma's fighting for their rights.

NO MORE WAR PLEASE
Is her message, emblazoned way up there in red
But it won't be seen by Mervyn
His war is over – he is dead.

Nance Cookson

Injustice on Justice (In = not Justice = just)

Not just! You cry.
How well we know the meaning of
Justice.
How well
injustice.
Perhaps they mean
the same.
Right is might? Wrong!
Wrong is might!
Yield and get
clobbered.
Confront –
same outcome.

Go
underground,
infiltrate,
move with
stealth. Until
the head of justice
begins to rise again.
What is nurtured, grows.
So too with Justice

Stand by with watering can and fertiliser.

Margo Poirier

Song of Athenian Gypsies

They occupy the periphery,
winter in wind-bitten alleys,
summer in panting diesel-heat
under hospitable plane trees.

You observe them unobtrusively,
drink in their colours wistfully –
swirls of flamingo and cochineal,
silver and lime, rose and violet.

They move with the grace of acrobats,
slender girls with tik-tak heels,
like wildflowers in gaudy fields
desired, devoid of coquetry.

Children of children raised
on the street, with incessant
sirens to lull them to sleep,
scorned and bedraggled, grubby,
streetwise, confront you with passion
and blame in their eyes – too unlike you
to feel comfortable with, in their vivid,
tenacious, precarious lives.

Jena Woodhouse

Chloe

It's as if we'd come to know you,
seeing your photo over and over
in newspapers or on TV.
You are alone and opening gifts,
drawn by your dolls pram down the street
or finally out in your garden.
It should have been a safe and quiet place
but you'd been forced
into the grasp of a motorbike,
pitting your strength against it,
wrestling with it and coming off worst.
We'll never forget the tumble of curls,
the wild gold ringlets about your head.
Your eyes were keen and questioning.
And filed away in our memory
another image of you, arms clasped
on your breast, right hand over left,
and as if self-taught and in doubt,
sensing the end of things,
accepting the nightfall of your heart.

Elaine Barker

Lost Voices

Thirty five years as a Public Servant.
I took my job seriously,
Considered myself a servant of the public.

Helped the voices of the public,
To be heard, to be acknowledged,
To not be taken for granted.

In today's world it seems,
Only those with the power,
The money or fame are heard.

What about everyone else?
The refugees, detainees, indigenous populations,
The frail, elderly, those with mental illnesses…

Who is helping them
To tell their stories,
To enable them to be heard?

There are laws in place
To stop voices, in the name of privacy,
Commercial in confidence, national security…

To what end
A secrecy agreement
Another one of these silencing laws?

Whistle-blowers
Tell stories not meant to be heard,
Tell stories that need to be heard.

Annette Jolly

Disability/invisibility

The pressing of a thousand bodies; a thousand voices
whispering in your ears like banshees on speed –
ecstatic werewolves licking your cheeks; tasting salt
as a precursor to saltier blood. Fangs and eyes.
Escape clawed dread through the door;
hide yourself from the crowd. Your heart,
a pink moth of muscle flutter fl flutt er
subsides into rhythm. The pack outside
can be heard, but screams become words
become murmurs. You clutch yourself to yourself
repeating the mantras: *your panic will subside –*
it's like the tide. Your panic is subsiding. Your salt lake panic
will soon evaporate; leaving only memory. Breathe!

Hands shaking slightly, you emerge, to join in,
to go back amongst people, where once
there were nightmares, riding you like mad jockeys.
A smug woman, radiating rules in a wire halo,
armed in her pale pink suit, addresses you (sotto voce):
That's the disabled toilet. You're not disabled.
Where's your wheelchair?
And you want to say, *my wheelchair is spinning*
through my brain; chemicals engaging smoothly,
synapses running gently downhill.
My wheelchair is invisible!
But you don't, in case, just in case,
she thinks that you may be a little cracked.

P.S. Cottier

They Came From Elsewhere

Nomads wanderers and lost souls
war and famine licking at their heels.
Trans migratory souls wandering
with maps in their heads
seeking borderless countries
for reincarnation elsewhere.
Outcasts with unanswered questions
from political faces, known or unknown.
The waters between seep into their minds
with long dark streets of razor wire
and leaky boats.
Their children watching, as words fall backwards
from political mouths.

Lorna Thrift Brooks

Asylum Seekers

With apologies to William Blake

To see a world in detention sand
And heaven in an excised flower
To hold a visa in your hand
And eternity in a Tampa hour.

To see children in a desert cage
Mothers wounded lacking care
Might put heaven in a rage
It leaves little mark elsewhere.

For they are forced to travel light
Chasing land beyond the sun
Trapped within their endless flight
And distant cries of Babylon.

In this new world they stand alone
Tormented by its unjust law
Downtrodden by the bloodless stone
And swept beneath its fatal shore.

Ian McFarlane

The Branch

How to address the hollowness
That looks out
From an old friend's eyes?

Much is demanded of the observer
– far more than the one
Salvaging the desire.

Affiliations are catching. Just
Search your pockets; you'll find smoke
But – there'll be no fire!

Most of us are in this state
Of rehabilitation, constantly
Meeting another's danse macabre…

People of the earth, there is
A conspiracy to keep us
Leaning away from ourselves:

Believe in the universal petition. Learn
To look into a cripple's eyes
And say…I know you.

Stefanie Bennett

Generations Lost

'Darkness cannot drive out darkness; only light can do that.' –Martin Luther King Jr

The government of the day took
it seemed
those words
in literal sense
choose
the half-caste state, the lighter ones,
they said
they will assimilate

They came
and then
we scattered
like hens
in their fowl yard
but never running fast enough
to beat them
to us

our Dreaming
those things
best forgotten
they said
white religion
better than darkness
but I am lost now
in the lightness of my skin and
all the forgotten languages

Myra King

Fruit Pickers Calling

Our calls
echo everywhere
Agnus Dei
we are not always paid
save grudgingly
while forced to exist
bereft of hope
graded lowest
in a sunburnt country
living like battery hens
in spaces undisclosed
by advertising

picking
in seasonal insecurity
Miserere Nobis
from the ends of the earth
hear our voices
among the trees
we stripped of fruit
give us a fair go.

Adrian Rogers

Down the Rabbit Hole With Alice

Can social justice live
When emotive words are edited
Out of the heart and soul of language
Leaving the dry husks?

We are left with
Jargonese
Facebook terminology
Techno-speak
Trendi-speak
And political correctness.

The needy words
that pertain to people's screaming
that need to stand up, be listened to
are as if surgically removed.

Social media dominated by
Happy pictures and happy news,
Liking, not liking, friending, unfriending.
Ready-made graphics, lingering for fleeting seconds in the mind,
Shared around with hundreds of friends never met,
Forever young, perfectly composed and socially correct,
And spamming for their on line business,
If not spamming obscenities out of malice.

There is no space left for going
Down the rabbit hole with Alice.

Adriana Wood

With the Dusk

With the dusk comes contemplation,
the orange-red sky is a canopy,
a tent.

Black against it rises,
the great, sleeping shoulder of a giant,
trees clinging to it like hair.
Along its belly the cars travel,
like fireflies in single file.
We are so small,
how can we be so terrible, such despoilers,
such monsters of cruelty?

The giant sleeps on until the end of time,
and we travel on, in single file, asleep at the wheel,
in love with our illusions.

Antonia Hildebrand

The Woman from the Shelter House

the woman from the shelter house
lives on the same street

in the playground
her children watch out for bear traps
amidst the climbing ropes

their sandpit
has turned to quicksand

behind the breakages of her eyes
her trust and beliefs have been stolen

and the words

that gather along the edge of her mouth
remain unspoken

while the space between her and others is
slammed shut

on the way home her children play
hide and seek
among the street trees

all their escape plans are well rehearsed

Jules Leigh Koch

Tutu's Fragments

South African Truth and Reconciliation Commission
Archbishop Desmond Tutu's London audience, 1999

Let's take off our shoes
We're on holy ground.

All they wanted was
To know the grave and say,
This is my brother
Yes, I know it's him.

I bought him those shoes.
They used orange wire
And the farm generator
To electrify his genitals.

Translators trapped
In the first-person cages
Of killers' minds
And victims' anguish know

Evil has nothing to do
With skin colour or race –
They do, we do
Succumb to evil

But God is good
He brought us closure

Ann Nadge

Misogynist Myth

It is written –
Of the ten parts of desire
Women possess nine,
So dangerous – they must be
Covered and controlled,
Lest they tempt weak men
With a glance or lock of hair.

Aren't men said to be
The stronger sex?

These men – who have only
One part of desire –
Why do they touch,
Proposition, abuse and rape,
Then blame women for their
Lack of self-control?

Avoid inflaming female passions,
Let men hide their bodies
From the lustful gaze of women

Jill Nevile

The Eyes Have It

Those dark eyes of haunted men
back streets of Paris, 1974,
survivors of Algeria's War of Independence
France unwelcoming
their language murmured only among themselves
their children changing their names to sound more French
Arabic cast out at interviews

These dark eyes of haunted men
Peeping from dark lanes, urine stench
Haunt me still

Not the Paris
The tourist seeks

Alice Shore

Mental Illness – its vagaries

Wellness returns
calm, contented,
safe, secure

confidence appears
medication forsaken
regression occurs

employment erodes
professionals alerted
medication begins

wellness returns
discretion enacted
calm and cautious

judiciously employed
capable – competent
unwound – unworried

cautiously calm
continued support
as needs require

early recognition
safety and security

Brenda Malcolm

That Box For Bones

People of Aboriginal descent are respectfully advised that this poem contains the name of a deceased person.

from a rattling old red country train
on some humid sixties summer's day
we visited the Melbourne Museum
Mother herding us to a foyer
the final stable for a racehorse
that lifted hearts out of depression:
behind glass in a smaller showcase
stood an exhibit stark in memory
its wood dark in polish – hard in grain
holding a human spine and ribcage
unlike Phar Lap, no hint of cover
to hide a taxidermist's stuffing
that box for bones no kind of coffin

Tasmania's last full-blood, Mum said...
after rape by whites – as I've since read –
she was brought to help quell Melbourne's blacks:
her group of five sought revenge instead –
for killing whalers her menfolk hanged
not free to speak in their own defence...
confined for life on Flinders Island
she begged to be buried out at sea:
still Truganini's corpse was exhumed
her hair and skin kept as specimens
by the Royal College of Surgeons –
she had to wait one hundred winters
for ashes on waves from her birthplace

Rodney Williams

Social Justice?

The quality of justice, including mercy,
is the greatest one of all.
But with its many transgressions,
it has become the one most likely
to be torn apart and fall.

Human error is tempting –
the precipice upon which we stand
is rocky and precarious.
Struggle for equality, to fight for what is right,
these are the only weapons.

Refugees felt sure of a welcome here
in this country lauded for compassion.
They risked their lives, braved the seas,
were forced into a kind of slavery
like animals in a zoo.

And also 'not like us'
there are many shunned by absurd excuses
enslaving those who fall in love
and wish to marry
labelled into categories of 'queer', or 'gay'.

New ways of thinking
Putting injustice to rout.
Could the 'yous' and the 'mes' bring that about?

Bobbie Barclay

Honour

While Sylvia tells her story
Her bolts of black hair, Iberian eyes
And orchid-petal lips
Embroider interwoven threads from an ancient past

Where myths of gods and goblins
Enfolded in zelkova woods, flamed crimson maple leaves
And shrouding morning mists
Leap and weave with her ancestral truth

For in Akizuki castle
Her mother's forebear, sword master to the lord
Was asked to gift his daughter
As signet to a Portuguese

I see the beauty of the daughter
And the strong strategic suitor for her hand
The imperious lord, the anguished father
The fearful followers of the master Samurai

For to gift the girl to such a one
Was family shame thereafter to purity of blood
Righted by duty absolute for the repair of honour
By ritual seppuku
And for Junshi, his Samurai to die as well

She tells the story with a blink of horror
She has imagined well the bath, the meal, the white death cloth
The inked death poem
And then the tanto knife quick gutting out each life

For honour and love
For family and lord
For what an ancient world believed was just.

Tracey-Anne Forbes

Celebrating May Day

Istanbul

The sea is dark and fierce
which Jason sailed
taking Medea from her Amazon country
back to a strange land
where men ruled

Grey-haired companions
My penfriend and I sit sipping tea
sheltered from cold and wind
and watch the twilight fall across the bay

Our talk is of sons
of sad and terrible things
we do not have the power to prevent

We tremble
and fear that we have lost our joy

But in the city
that same evening
jeans-clad maidens
walk the red flag forest
long hair streaming
beating drums
holding hands and dancing

No War   Peace Now
they shout
End Women's Slavery
Long Live May Day

and all is young again

Eileen Haley

When My Eyes No Longer See

Dusk creeps on the shore.
Children pack
Balls buckets and blankets into
Large sand-covered bags.

Older, young people arrive.
A whiff of pizza
Wafts across my nose
I hear the clink of glass on glass
And the muted sound
of modern music.

As the last sliver of sun
Slips over the horizon,
Dark shapeless humps
Become random dots along the shore.

What will I see, when my eyes no longer see?
Will some other sense compensate?
Like Zeus's gift of clairvoyance
To Tiresias? Or will the gods clean my
Ears and birdsong will be
enchantingly clearer?

Like the ancient Greek might have done,
I sit in the fading light
Watching memories made in the sunlight
Of earlier years to lighten my heart.
I tighten my fist around a white
Guiding pole and wait to be rescued.

Rose Helen Mitchell

What Happened?

London, January 1969, our Pakistani landlord said,
'You can't keep that newborn baby here…'

Dublin, December 1969 my Irish in-laws said,
'We don't want you and your newborn baby here…'

Buckinghamshire, June 1970, my parents said,
'You and your babies can't stay here
It's your husband's responsibility to provide you with a home.'

We had become outcasts in our homelands
Because we wanted a place to raise our children
Where racial and religious intolerance
Would not make impossible
Dreams of a bright future for them

Adelaide, November 1970, the Good Neighbour movement said,
'Welcome to Australia…'

When I tell my story I am applauded
For leaving everything familiar
To make a new beginning

What happened in Australia
That today the plight of refugees
Is worse than mine had been
And we do not welcome those
Whose homelands we have helped destroy?

Brenda Eldridge

Afterword

Over the last twenty years, it has been my privilege to publish several hundred books by new and established Australian poets. The authors of many of those books, from almost every year of Ginninderra Press's history, are represented in this collection skilfully and sensitively edited by Ann Nadge.

Poets seeking to have their work published by Ginninderra Press are informed that 'Manuscripts should combine emotional impact with arresting imagery. Social awareness is also looked on favourably.' This collection testifies most especially, of course, to the social awareness of Ginninderra Press poets and I'm heartened to find that so many writers share my passion for social justice in all its expressions and have been willing to share that passion.

First Refuge is, I think, a powerful collection that not only reflects the current social concerns of a cross-section of Australian writers but also works to celebrate the place – dare I say the importance – of independent publishing in a cultural scene dominated by mass markets and the superficial gloss of celebrity. What a wonderful way to mark Ginninderra Press's twentieth birthday!

Stephen Matthews

www.ingramcontent.com/pod-product-compliance
Lightning Source LLC
Chambersburg PA
CBHW070048120526
44589CB00034B/1603